MY FIRST BRITANNICA

Birds, Insects, Reptiles,
and Aquatic Life

11

ENCYCLOPÆDIA
Britannica®

CHICAGO   LONDON   NEW DELHI   PARIS   SEOUL   SYDNEY   TAIPEI   TOKYO

International Standard Book Number: 1-59339-048-3 (set)
International Standard Book Number: 1-59339-059-9 (volume 11)

My First Britannica:
Volume 11: Birds, Insects, Reptiles, and Aquatic Life 2004

Britannica.com may be accessed on the Internet at http://www.britannica.com.

Birds, Insects, Reptiles, and Aquatic Life

TABLE OF CONTENTS

Great white shark
© Amos Nachoum/Corbis

Birds, Insects, Reptiles, and Aquatic Life

INTRODUCTION

How did the 'dabbler duck' get its name?

Do snakes chew their food? What insect might survive a nuclear bomb blast?

Is a sponge a plant or an animal?

In Volume 11, *Birds, Insects, Reptiles, and Aquatic Life,* you'll discover answers to these questions and many more. Through pictures, articles, and fun facts, you'll learn about the great diversity of animal life found around the world.

To help you on your journey, we've provided the following signposts in *Birds, Insects, Reptiles, and Aquatic Life*:

■ **Subject Tabs**—The coloured box in the upper corner of each right-hand page will quickly tell you the article subject.

■ **Search Lights**—Try these mini-quizzes before and after you read the article and see how much - *and how quickly* - you can learn. You can even make this a game with a reading partner. (Answers are upside down at the bottom of one of the pages.)

■ **Did You Know?**—Check out these fun facts about the article subject. With these surprising 'factoids', you can entertain your friends, impress your teachers, and amaze your parents.

■ **Picture Captions**—Read the captions that go with the photos. They provide useful information about the article subject.

■ **Vocabulary**—New or difficult words are in **bold type**. You'll find them explained in the Glossary at the back of this volume. And there's a complete listing of all Glossary terms in the set in the **Reference Guide and Index**, Volume 13.

■ **Learn More!**—Follow these pointers to related articles throughout the set.

And don't forget: If you're not sure where to start, where you saw something before, or where to go next, the **Reference Guide and Index** (Volume 13) will point the way.

Have a great trip!

MY FIRST BRITANNICA

What
do birds
have that no
other animal has?

DID YOU KNOW?

A few birds have a curious trick of stroking their feathers with live ants. It's not clear why they do this. One explanation is that an acid produced by the ants seems to kill or drive away insects.

Birds of a Feather

Like many animals, birds are **warm-blooded**. They have many other features in common with other animals, too. But they have one feature that makes them **unique** among all living animals: birds have feathers.

The entire covering of feathers is called the bird's 'plumage'. Feathers are an important part of why most birds can fly. And feathers help protect all birds from rain, cold, and heat.

The next time it rains, watch for birds outside the window. You may see them standing with wings and tail drooping to the ground. The water simply slides off without soaking through. On a cold winter day you may notice that birds fluff out their feathers. Fluffed-out feathers hold a layer of warm air next to the skin. In hot weather a bird flattens its feathers. This keeps the skin cool by stopping hot air from reaching it.

Birds have different kinds of feathers. In many birds a thick coat of feathers called 'down' lies closest to the skin. Down feathers are soft and warm. Water birds have extra-thick coats of down. That's one reason why ducks can paddle about in icy winter waters without getting cold. A bird's main body feathers are called '**contour** feathers'. Most contour feathers have many small hooks. The tiny hooks lock together like a zip, which makes the feathers smooth in a single direction. Some contour feathers are colourful and are for show only. Other contour feathers are special 'flight feathers'. These are found on the edges and tips of the wing and in the tail. They can be adjusted as a bird flies to help the bird steer and change speed.

LEARN MORE! READ THESE ARTICLES…
AIRPLANES (VOLUME 2) • BATS (VOLUME 12)
MAMMALS (VOLUME 12)

Answer: Birds are the only living animals to have feathers.

SEARCH LIGHT

Find and correct the error in the following sentence: The most commonly seen kingfisher in North America is the kookaburra.

Laugh, Kookaburra!

The birds known as kingfishers are found all over the world, but most kinds live in **tropical** areas. Many kingfishers are brightly coloured, especially the ones found in Southeast Asia. All are famous for their swift dives.

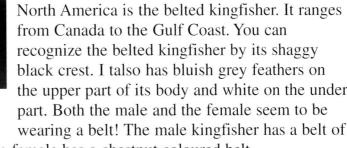

(Top) Sacred kingfisher; (bottom) Malachite kingfisher.

Kingfishers are often boldly patterned. Many of them have **crests** on their large heads. Their bodies are squat, and their bills are long and heavy. A kingfisher's long bill helps it to catch fish as it swoops into the water.

The most commonly spotted kingfisher in North America is the belted kingfisher. It ranges from Canada to the Gulf Coast. You can recognize the belted kingfisher by its shaggy black crest. I talso has bluish grey feathers on the upper part of its body and white on the under part. Both the male and the female seem to be wearing a belt! The male kingfisher has a belt of grey breast feathers. The female has a chestnut coloured belt.

The belted kingfisher makes its nest in a hole that it digs in the ground close to streams and lakes. The nest is full of fish bones. The belted kingfisher eats only fish, which it catches. Once the fish has been caught, the kingfisher whacks it against a branch a few times and then eats it whole!

Some kingfishers live in forests rather than near water. Among the forest kingfishers is the well known kookaburra of Australia. It eats reptiles, including poisonous snakes. The kookaburra is sometimes called the '**bushman's** clock', because it is heard early in the morning and just after sunset. It has a loud laughing or **braying** voice.

LEARN MORE! READ THESE ARTICLES…
AUSTRALIA (VOLUME 7) • FISH (VOLUME 11)
KANGAROOS (VOLUME 12)

DID YOU KNOW?

A pair of belted kingfishers will take turns digging a tunnel into a riverbank to create their nest. They dig with their bills and use their feet to kick the loose dirt from the tunnel's mouth.

Answer: The most commonly seen kingfisher in North America is the belted kingfisher.

Bright Colours and Brilliant Whites

Parrots and cockatoos have long fascinated humans. These lively birds not only are beautiful but they entertain us with their chatter and behaviour as well. Many parrots are brightly coloured, with green feathers and patches of red, orange, or blue. Most cockatoos are white, and all have a patch of long feathers called a 'crest' on their head that stands up straight when the bird is excited.

Citron-crested cockatoo.
© Eric and David Hosking/Corbis

Parrots and cockatoos belong to the same family as cockatiels, macaws, parakeets, and many other colourful birds. The tiniest parrot is the pygmy parrot, which is only 7 centimetres long. The largest member of the family is a type of macaw that can be as much as 101 centimetres long.

All the birds in this family have strong hooked bills that can crack open nuts. Their thick fleshy tongues help them eat. Some birds have brush-tipped tongues that are useful in sucking **nectar** from flowers and juice from fruits.

Parrots and cockatoos have unusual feet. Two toes point forward and two point backward. This lets them climb trees swiftly and grasp their food firmly as they eat it. The birds can also use their strong bills to help them climb.

Parrots and cockatoos are found in most **tropical** regions of the world, especially in rainforests. These birds can live for 30 to 50 years. Some have been known to live for 80 years!

Some parrots talk, sing, laugh, and whistle. They have a sharp sense of hearing and can **echo** human sounds and speech. Cockatoos can talk too. They are very **impish** and like to play tricks - like figuring out how to escape from their cages!

LEARN MORE! READ THESE ARTICLES...
AMAZON: A CLOSE LOOK AT RIVER LIFE (VOLUME 9)
BIRDS (VOLUME 11) • RAINFORESTS (VOLUME 1)

SEARCH LIGHT

Fill in the gaps: Parrots and cockatoos have unusual feet, with _____ pointing forward and _____ pointing backward.

Macaws gather at Manu National Park in Peru to eat clay. The clay adds minerals to the birds' diet.
© Michael & Patricia Fogden/Corbis

DID YOU KNOW?

Like many rainforest animals, wild parrots are endangered. This is partly because their homes are destroyed when the forest is cut down or burned. But they are also threatened by people who hunt them in order to sell them as pets.

Answer: Parrots and cockatoos have unusual feet, with two toes pointing forward and two toes pointing backward.

DID YOU KNOW?
Owls swallow their food whole, and then afterward they cough up hard balls of the parts they can't eat, such as bones and fur. If you find these hairy lumps scattered under a tree, it's a pretty good bet there's an owl nearby.

The Nighttime Hunters

Maybe it's because they fly mostly at night that owls seem so mysterious. Some **superstitions** connect them with scary things such as witches. But owls aren't that mysterious, and they aren't scary. They are simply **nocturnal** birds. And they are very helpful to people.

Saw-whet owls.
Ron Austing—Frank Lane Picture Agency/Corbis

Owls are hunters. Some owls eat insects or fish, but most eat rodents, such as mice and rats. Without owls, there would be too many rodents, and rodents are serious **pests.**

Owls can see better at night than most animals. They have excellent hearing and can detect the smallest scratchings of a mouse. When it comes to locating **prey**, their hearing helps them more than their eyesight. Because of their soft feathers, owls fly silently and almost always surprise their prey. Owls catch their prey in their long strong claws and swallow it without chewing.

The only way an owl can look around is to turn its head. It can turn its head almost all the way around, turning it so fast that you can hardly see it move. Sometimes it looks as though the owl is turning its head all the way around in a full circle!

Some people say owls are wise. That is because they were once associated with Athena, the Greek goddess of wisdom.

Owls sleep during the day, hidden among tree branches. If you were to see an owl, you'd probably mistake it for a piece of bark. It would sit still, not moving a feather. It wouldn't even move its eyes. It couldn't, because an owl's eyes can't move! This is why owls seem to stare at you - if you're lucky enough to see one!

LEARN MORE! READ THESE ARTICLES...
BATS (VOLUME 12) • BIRDS (VOLUME 11) • EAGLES (VOLUME 11)

Common barn owls live all over the world, except in Antarctica and Micronesia.
© Eric and David Hosking/Corbis

SEARCH LIGHT

Why do some people think that owls can turn their heads all the way around in a circle?

Answer: Owls can turn their heads to the left or the right almost all the way around. It's because the head snaps back so quickly, truly in the blink of an eye, that people think owls can turn their heads all the way around.

Riders of the Wind

If an eagle spread its wings in your room, it would take up as much space as your bed. Eagles have been called the 'king of birds' because of their **majestic** appearance and power of flight. They fly easily, using air currents to ride the wind.

Eagles are birds of prey, which means that they hunt other animals for food. One reason they are such good hunters is that they have excellent

Golden eagle.
© Royalty-Free/Corbis

eyesight. Even when an eagle is so high in the air that it can hardly be seen, it can still see small objects on the ground. When it spots a meal, it swoops down and grabs the animal with its strong claws. Then it uses its hooked beak to tear the animal apart.

Eagles build huge nests of sticks on rocky cliffs or in the treetops. Their nests are big enough to hold people! Eagles use the same nest year after year, returning to it with the same mate.

When there are eggs to hatch, both the mother and the father eagles take turns sitting on them. Both parents care for the little eagles afterward, taking them mice, fish, rabbits, ducks, snakes, and squirrels to eat. But eagles don't always catch their own food. Sometimes they steal food from another bird by chasing the bird until it gets tired and drops whatever it is carrying.

Not all eagles look alike. A golden eagle has a cap of gold feathers on its head. A bald eagle is not really bald, but it looks that way because its head feathers are white and its body feathers are brown.

LEARN MORE! READ THESE ARTICLES…
BIRDS (VOLUME 11) • NORTH AMERICA (VOLUME 9)
RABBITS (VOLUME 12)

DID YOU KNOW?
When eagles choose a mate, they do a dramatic high-flying act called cartwheeling. Gripping each other with their claws, they plunge together toward the ground. At the last moment they pull apart and fly upward again.

Near Kenai, Alaska, a bald eagle perches on a branch.
© Theo Allofs/Corbis

SEARCH LIGHT

Find and correct the error in the following sentence: Only female eagles take care of the babies.

Answer: Both male and female eagles take care of the babies.

SEARCH LIGHT

Which of the following can be said about an albatross?
a) It spends most of its time on land.
b) It eats other birds.
c) It goes to land only to lay eggs.

Albatrosses use their long wings to soar and glide on air currents. They can stay in the air for hours without flapping their wings. The black-browed albatross, shown here in flight, has a dark marking around the eye that makes it look as though it is frowning.

Forever Gliding

The albatross is an amazing seabird. It spends most of its life soaring above the water. The only time albatrosses ever go ashore is when they lay eggs and raise their chicks. Groups (called 'colonies') of the birds build nests on isolated Antarctic islands. A single large white egg is laid in a bowl-shaped nest built from plants and soil. Sometimes the nest is just a patch of bare ground.

Scientists measuring an albatross' wingspread.
© Wolfgang Kaehler/Corbis

A young albatross grows slowly. It takes at least four months for it to develop all the feathers it will need to fly. Once it's able to fly, the albatross will spend the next five to ten years out at sea. The albatross can glide for days at a time, without flapping its long narrow wings. To stay in the air like this, it needs windy weather. In calm weather the albatross has trouble keeping its heavy body in the air, so it rests on the water and floats like a cork. It feeds on small **squid** and fish. But it will also follow fishing boats and eat scraps that are thrown overboard.

Some kinds of albatrosses are brown, but most of them are white with some brown or black markings on their bodies or wings. Albatrosses are the largest of all flying birds. In fact, the wandering albatross has the largest wingspread amongst living birds. The wings of a wandering albatross can measure 3.4 metres from tip to tip.

Albatrosses live very long lives and are one of the few species of bird that die of old age.

LEARN MORE! READ THESE ARTICLES…
AIRPLANES (VOLUME 2) • GULLS (VOLUME 11) • INDIAN OCEAN (VOLUME 1)

DID YOU KNOW?

In the past, sailors believed albatrosses had special powers. They believed that killing the bird would bring bad luck.

Answer: c) It goes to land only to lay eggs.

Gulls are among the most common water birds of ocean and coastal zones worldwide. Some gulls travel enormous distances between their summer and winter homes.

SEARCH LIGHT

How are gulls helpful to humans?

The Ocean's Clean-up Crew

A fishing boat chugs back into the harbour with its day's catch. The gulls follow close behind. They know that the fishermen will be throwing treats overboard as they empty the bait bag and clean the deck. The gulls dip into the waves to scoop up bits of food. They fill the air with their excited cries. This often happens when they are fighting over something good to eat.

Along the shore, gulls are helpful to the people who clean beaches and harbours. They swoop down to pick up messy things. Gulls eat almost anything, from dead fish to crisps and scraps of hot dogs. And they clear away lots of insects too.

Gulls eat all day long. They have to just to stay alive. Gulls are big birds that fly great distances. While flying, they use up a lot of energy. Gulls can fly many kilometres without stopping. They can fly from one end of a country to the other. But all the time they're up there, they're looking down to see if they can find something to eat.

Seagull stands on a rock.
© Guy Motil/Corbis

Gulls are good swimmers too. Their feet are webbed. The little stretches of skin between their toes make their feet act as paddles.

Gulls are also floaters. They stay on top of the water like a piece of wood does. On long trips over the ocean, they drop down onto the water and float while taking a nap.

LEARN MORE! READ THESE ARTICLES…
FISH (VOLUME 11) • OCEANS (VOLUME 1) • SHIPS (VOLUME 2)

DID YOU KNOW?
The type of gull called Bonaparte's gull was named after Charles-Lucien Bonaparte, a nephew of the famous French emperor Napoleon Bonaparte. The younger Bonaparte spent much of his life studying the world's birds.

Answer: Gulls clean up a lot of food waste from beaches, harbours, picnic areas, tips, and car parks that would otherwise be left behind as rubbish.

DID YOU KNOW?
Ducks make their feathers waterproof by rubbing oil on them. They get the oil from special glands on their chests and rub it on their feathers with their bills.

A male wood duck is easily identifiable by his purple and green head, his reddish-brown breast flecked with white, and his bronze sides.
© Gary W. Carter/Corbis

SEARCH LIGHT

Unscramble these words that have to do with a duck.
wsmimre
nblbiadg
dlwaed

Dabblers, Divers, and Perchers

Ducks are champion swimmers and are at home almost anywhere near water. Some feed and nest in streams and ponds. Others live near deep wide lakes. Some make their homes on rocky cliffs by the ocean.

There are three kinds of duck:

'**Dabbling** ducks' put their heads under water to eat plants that grow there. This way of feeding is called 'dabbling'. They build their nests in hollows near the water. There they also eat plants and insects found near the shore. Dabbling ducks can fly very fast.

'Diving ducks' dive deep down into the water to find things to eat. They mostly eat fish. They are very strong swimmers.

'Perching ducks' make nests in trees and hold on to the branches with their long-clawed toes. This is called perching. Some may perch on the tall stalks that grow over marshy ponds.

All ducks are graceful fliers and swimmers. But on the ground they waddle from side to side, moving slowly in a funny, jerky way. You usually don't see a duck waddling too far away from water.

(Top) A dabbling gadwall duck; (bottom) young girl holding a fluffy duckling.

In winter many ducks fly south, where the water is warmer and there's more to eat. But icy cold water doesn't bother them. A thick inner layer of soft fluffy feathers called 'down' keeps them warm. And their bigger outer feathers help too. They're **waterproof**. Feathers are a duck's raincoat. Every year ducks lose their old feathers, and new feathers grow in. This is called 'moulting'. Until the new feathers grow, ducks can't fly. So they hide in the grass or on the water to keep safe from enemies.

LEARN MORE! READ THESE ARTICLES...
GEESE (VOLUME 11) • MARSHES (VOLUME 1) • OCEANS (VOLUME 1)

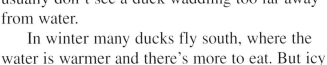

Answer: wsnimre = swimmer
nblibadg = dabbling
dlwaed = waddle

Fine-Feathered Travellers

Geese are found virtually everywhere. There's the wild Canada goose, and halfway around the world is the snow goose of Siberia. There is the **pied** goose, which lives 'down under' in Australia. The rarely seen Hawaiian goose lives out in the middle of the Pacific Ocean. The little brant goose nests in very cold Arctic areas. The wild goose called the greylag is found in Europe.

Geese spend a lot of time in the water. Like ducks, they have a coat of oil on their feathers that keeps them from getting too wet. And the soft feathers beneath, called 'down', keep them warm even in the iciest of waters. Down is so good at keeping things warm that people often use it in ski jackets and in duvets. It's also good in pillows because it's so soft.

(Top) Mother goose nuzzling her gosling (young goose); (bottom) snow geese flying in a V formation.

Geese are fairly large birds, often standing a metre tall despite their short legs. Geese may look somewhat silly when they waddle on land. But their **sturdy** legs actually help them walk more steadily than ducks or swans do.

Geese have webbed feet that make them strong swimmers. They are also powerful fliers. They can make especially long flights during their annual **migrations** to their winter feeding grounds. You may see groups of geese travelling south in the autumn in lines that make a V shape. This formation helps keep them from getting tired as they fly because each goose gets a lift from the air flowing off the goose ahead.

LEARN MORE! READ THESE ARTICLES…
CANADA (VOLUME 9) • DUCKS (VOLUME 11)
EUROPE (VOLUME 6)

DID YOU KNOW?
Some people keep geese as guards. Geese make loud honking cries when danger appears. After chasing the enemy away, they cackle triumphantly.

SEARCH LIGHT

How
do people
use
down feathers?

A Canada goose flies close to the water.

Answer: People use down to stuff pillows, duvets, and ski jackets because the feathers are soft and very warm.

Birds of Beauty, Grace, and Speed

Ducks, geese, and swans are the three main kinds of waterfowl. Swans are the largest of the three, and they are also the fastest flyers and swimmers. They have a stately and dignified appearance when swimming on a pond.

Like the other waterfowl, swans have oily feathers that stay dry in the water. Their webbed feet make them strong swimmers. Swans are heavy-bodied birds that feed by dabbling - dipping the long neck into shallow water for plants. They don't dive for food. They have powerful wings for flying long distances.

Mother swan and cygnets.
© AFP/Corbis

The whistling swan and the trumpeter swan are found in North America, while the mute swan lives in Europe and Asia. These birds are white. South America is the home of the black-necked swan, while the beautiful black swan lives in Australia. It is the state emblem of Western Australia.

Swans make a variety of sounds. Even the mute swan often hisses or makes soft snoring sounds. It may even grunt sharply.

The male swan is called a 'cob'. The female is called a 'pen'. They look alike. A pair of swans usually stays together for life. The female swan lays about six pale eggs on a heap of plant material, while the male keeps close guard. The young swans are called 'cygnets'. They can run and swim just a few hours after they hatch. But father and mother swan look after them carefully for several months. Sometimes the cygnets will ride on their mother's back when they get tired from swimming or need protection from enemies.

LEARN MORE! READ THESE ARTICLES...
DUCKS (VOLUME 11) • GEESE (VOLUME 11)
WESTERN AUSTRALIA (VOLUME 7)

DID YOU KNOW?
E.B. White's *The Trumpet of the Swan* is a story about a voiceless swan that learns to play a trumpet.

SEARCH LIGHT

What's one way that ducks and swans are alike? How are they different?

A family of mute swans, with cygnets riding on their mother's back, swim along the water.
© Philip Perry—Frank Lane Picture Agency/Corbis

Answer: Both ducks and swans are water birds with oily feathers and webbed feet for swimming. But swans are considerably bigger than ducks. They fly and swim faster than ducks too.

Penguins are excellent divers and swimmers. Here, gentoo penguins enjoy a romp through the water.

SEARCH LIGHT

Do penguins have feathers?

Well-Dressed Swimmers

When a penguin swims, its light-coloured belly and dark-coloured back help hide it from enemies. From underneath, its light belly looks like the sky. This makes it hard for its enemy the leopard seal to see it. From above, its dark back looks like the dark water, which helps hide it from big hunting birds.

Members of the emperor penguin species, the largest of the penguins.
© Tim Davis/Corbis

Penguins cannot fly, but they swim extremely well. The shape of their bodies, sort of like a submarine, lets them swim very fast. They use their short flat wings like flippers and practically fly through the water. In fact, they often leap out of the water and look as if they are trying to flap through the air.

There are 17 types of penguins. They live in Antarctica and along the cool portions of the coasts of Africa, New Zealand, Australia, and South America. Penguins have a thick layer of fat that helps to protect them from the cold. And although they don't look like they do, they actually have feathers all over their bodies. These short feathers also help to keep them warm.

Penguins' short legs give them an odd walk. They do, however, run quickly. Sometimes they'll build up speed and then slide on their bellies to travel quickly over ice and snow.

Penguins live in nesting **colonies**. These colonies can be enormous. Penguins return to the same place, the same nest, and the same partner every year - sometimes travelling long distances. Penguins use the Sun to help them find their direction. Most penguins build a nest on the ground with pebbles, mud, and vegetation. The females lay one or two eggs, and then both parents take turns looking after them.

LEARN MORE! READ THESE ARTICLES…
ANTARCTICA (VOLUME 1) • BIRDS (VOLUME 11) • WALRUSES (VOLUME 12)

DID YOU KNOW?

Penguins are the only birds that can swim but not fly.

Answer: Like all birds, penguins have feathers. But theirs are so short and close to their bodies that the feathers look more like skin.

Proud Birds

A peacock's feathers are brilliant shades of bronze, blue, green, and gold. It even has a little crown of feathers, called a 'crest', on the top of its head. The centre of attraction, though, is the peacock's long tail. At the tip of each tail feather is a big shiny spot ringed with blue and bronze that looks like an eye.

When the male peacock wants to attract a female peacock (called a 'peahen'), it dances! And again the action is all in the tail. The peacock lifts its tail and spreads it out like a fan. Every feather is shown off this way. At the end of this show, the peacock makes its tail feathers **vibrate**. This makes the quills in the long tail feathers rattle and rustle. The peahen is charmed!

Peahens do not have long tails or crests. They are green and brown in colour and almost as big as the males.

Peacocks live in the wild in Southeast Asia and belong to the pheasant family. Two important kinds of peacock are the green, or Javanese, peacock and the blue, or Indian, peacock. The green peacock is found from Myanmar to Java. The blue is found in India and Sri Lanka. These beautiful birds can also be seen in zoos around the world.

A long time ago, people kept peacocks at home. The ancient Greeks called the peacock 'Hera's bird'. In their religion, Hera was the wife of Zeus, the god of sky and weather. She was thought of as the queen of heaven. According to an old story, the eyelike markings on peacock feathers were the 100 eyes of the giant Argus.

LEARN MORE! READ THESE ARTICLES...
BIRDS (VOLUME 11) • INDIA (VOLUME 7) • SRI LANKA (VOLUME 7)

SEARCH LIGHT

The male peacock in the picture is spreading his tail feathers to try to
a) scare the peahen.
b) attract the peahen.
c) hide the peahen.

The male peacock displays his feathers to get the attention of the female.
© Terry W. Eggers/Corbis

DID YOU KNOW?

Peacocks may be beautiful birds, but they definitely don't have beautiful voices. Peacocks make a harsh screeching when they 'sing', if you can call it that.

Answer: b) attract the peahen.

SEARCH LIGHT

Which of the following can be said about ostriches?
- Ostriches eat a lot of meat.
- Ostriches are the biggest bird.
- Ostriches are great runners.

The Biggest Birds in the World

The ostrich is the largest living bird in the world. Ostriches are about 2.5 metres tall and may weigh as much as 155 kilos. They have very short wings, which means ostriches are too heavy to fly. Ostriches' wings can't get them into the air, but flapping their wings while they run helps the birds go faster on the ground. Ostriches can run up to 65 kilometres an hour. This makes them not just the biggest but also the fastest bird on the ground!

Ostriches don't use their speed to catch food. Instead, they run to keep away from their enemies. But the first thing ostriches do when they see an enemy is hide. To avoid being seen, ostriches generally lie flat on the ground with their necks outstretched. This makes them look like just another bush. People sometimes say that ostriches bury their heads in the sand when they sense danger. But this isn't true. You just can't see their heads when ostriches are lying down.

Male ostrich protecting eggs in a nest.
© Kevin Schafer/Corbis

Ostriches don't always hide or run away from trouble. If their young are in danger, ostriches will fight. They use their beaks, and they kick with their very powerful legs. An ostrich could easily kill a person with a few kicks of its feet.

Wild ostriches live in groups in Africa. Sometimes there are as many as 50 birds in a single group. Ostriches eat mostly plants, fruits, and berries, but once in a while they'll also eat small animals and insects.

A tame ostrich that's been treated well may do a very special thing: it can be trained to carry people on its back. In fact, in some parts of the world people have ostrich races.

LEARN MORE! READ THESE ARTICLES…
AFRICA (VOLUME 8) • PEACOCKS (VOLUME 11)
PENGUINS (VOLUME 11)

DID YOU KNOW?
In the days when fashionable women wore very big hats, they were often decorated with ostrich feathers.

Answer: Ostriches are the biggest bird and are great runners too.

31

SEARCH LIGHT

Fill in
the gap:
The kiwi is an
unusual bird. Its
_____
are not fully formed,
so it does not fly.

New Zealand's Feathered Favourites

The kiwi is a strange little bird found only in the forests of the island nation of New Zealand. During the day it sleeps in its burrow, and at night it looks for food, as the one in the large photo is doing. Kiwis eat worms, insects, **larvae**, spiders, and berries.

Kiwis have a strong sense of smell and a touch-

'Kiwi crossing' road sign in New Zealand.
© Paul A. Souders/Corbis

sensitive bill. They are the only birds whose nostrils are at the very end of the bill. The kiwi's bill is long and narrow, and there are sensitive whiskers at the base of it. Having noses at the very end of their bills is a big help when they are hunting!

Kiwis also have a good sense of hearing, but they have poor vision in daylight. To escape enemies they rely on their strong legs. Kiwis are fast runners and fierce fighters. They have four toes on each foot, each with a large claw. The claws are very useful when kiwis are facing enemies.

The kiwi is an unusual bird. It is greyish brown and about as big as a chicken. It has wings that are not fully formed, so it does not fly. The wings are hidden in its feathers, which are shaggy and hair-like.

The bird is much loved by the people of New Zealand, even though they don't see it very often. New Zealanders themselves are sometimes called Kiwis. A fruit, a breakfast cereal, and an airline are named after the kiwi too. Pictures of the bird can be seen on New Zealand's postage stamps and coins.

DID YOU KNOW?
Compared with the size of the bird, the kiwi's egg isn't just large, it's enormous. The egg is about 20 per cent of the mother's weight. It fills almost her entire body right before it's laid.

LEARN MORE! READ THESE ARTICLES…
BIRDS (VOLUME 11) • NEW ZEALAND (VOLUME 7) • OSTRICHES (VOLUME 11)

Answer: The kiwi is an unusual bird. Its wings are not fully formed, so it does not fly.

Citizens of the Waters

A fish is a cold-blooded animal that has a backbone, lives in water, and breathes by means of **gills**. It normally has two pairs of fins in place of arms and legs, as well as several other fins. Most fish are covered with **scales**.

Fish are fascinating in their variety. The sea horse looks something like a tiny horse standing on its tail. Flounders are as flat as a dinner plate. The rabbitfish, a small relative of the shark, has a head and teeth resembling those of a rabbit. Anglerfish carry their own 'fishing rod' to catch other fish. An extended part of the back fin has wormlike pieces of flesh at the tip, which are the 'bait'. Anglers of the deep sea have bait that lights up to attract victims.

Size differs as much as shape. Some Philippine gobies reach an adult size of less than one and a quarter centimetres. The whale shark, the largest of all fishes, reaches 50 metres in length and weighs about 18 tonnes.

Fish swim mainly by sideways movements of the body and tail. The fins are used for balancing, steering, and braking. To move quickly from a resting position, some fish shoot a stream of water out of the gills, which causes them to lunge forward. The fastest swimmers, such as the tuna, can travel 48 kilometres per hour.

Most fish continue to grow as long as they live. Fish that live to an old age can become very large. Carp are among this group. They may live 100 years!

LEARN MORE! READ THESE ARTICLES...
GREAT BARRIER REEF (VOLUME 7) • RIVERS (VOLUME 1)
SHARKS (VOLUME 11)

DID YOU KNOW?
Fish called mudskippers can crawl across mud flats and wet fields in search of food. Lungfish can burrow into mud when their pools dry up. They lie there, for months if necessary, until rain refills the pools.

SEARCH LIGHT

Fill in
the gap.
Fish
breathe through
_____ .

Answer: Fish breathe through gills.

DID YOU KNOW?
The common goldfish, often a child's first pet, is a member of the carp family.

The Fishy Survivor

True or false? Carp live in the ocean.

The common carp is a fish that lives along the muddy bottoms of ponds, lakes, and rivers. It swallows plants, insects, and anything else it finds to eat. It was first found in Asia but was later taken into Europe and North America. Some people like to eat carp.

Sometimes carp can live 100 years and grow to weigh 35 kilos or more. But not all carp grow that old or that heavy. The fish that are caught usually are under 10 years old and do not weigh more than 4.5 kilos.

The carp has a blunt nose and a small thick-lipped mouth. From its upper lip dangle two pairs of feelers that are called 'barbels'.

There are three kinds of common carp. The scale carp has large scales all over its wide heavy body. Its back is olive green, its sides are gold-coloured, and its belly is bright yellow. The mirror carp has only three or four rows of huge scales along its sides. The leather carp is almost without scales, but it has a very thick skin.

In some ways the carp is a **nuisance**. In hunting for food, the carp muddies the water. This affects the life of many plants and animals. A carp sometimes pushes more valuable fish away from their food and also eats their eggs. The carp has a habit of pulling out plants from their roots. This keeps ducks away. It is very difficult to get rid of carp. The fish can thrive even in dirty water and can also survive in very warm and very cold water.

Goldfish swimming in a bowl.
© Doug Wilson/Corbis

LEARN MORE! READ THESE ARTICLES...
FISH (VOLUME 11) • GREAT LAKES (VOLUME 9) • RIVERS (VOLUME 1)

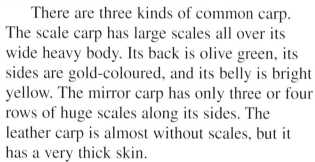

Colourful carp swim in a pond outside a restaurant in Japan. In Asia and Europe carp are often raised in ponds because it is possible to grow many fish in a small amount of water.
© Wolfgang Kaehler/Corbis

Answer: FALSE. They live in freshwater rivers, lakes, and ponds.

Leaping Up the Waterfall

SEARCH LIGHT

True or false? Salmon travel upstream against the river current to lay their eggs.

These fish aren't going down a waterfall. They're going up! Not much can stop these big strong salmon - not even a waterfall. The salmon are swimming up the river to return to the quiet waters where they hatched. They're returning in order to spawn - that is, to lay their own eggs. They started their journey far out in the sea.

Somehow the salmon manage to find the river they are looking for. Night and day they swim on. They eat nothing at all after getting into their river. Finally, they reach the waters where they came from.

Male sockeye salmon.
© Natalie Fobes/Corbis

We don't know how salmon can find their way on this long trip up the river. But we know what they do when they reach the end. At the top of the stream, the mother salmon digs a long hole with her tail and **snout**. She fills the hole with thousands of tiny eggs. She covers the eggs with sand to keep them safe.

The eggs hatch. When the baby salmon are about as long as your finger, they are big enough to start the swim to the ocean. They float backward down the long river - tails first and heads last! They seem to steer better that way.

Many of the babies never reach the ocean because there are too many enemies. Birds, bears, and bigger fish along the way love to eat them. The salmon that do reach the ocean will one day start the long hard trip up the river.

LEARN MORE! READ THESE ARTICLES...
AMERICAN INDIANS (VOLUME 4) • FISH (VOLUME 11) • RIVERS (VOLUME 1)

These Pacific salmon are trying to leap up a waterfall of the Brooks River in Katmai National Park, Alaska, U.S., to spawn upstream.
© Galen Rowell/Corbis

Answer: TRUE.

A Frightening Little Fish

The piranha is found in the rivers and lakes of South America. It is a meat-eating fish with long, triangular, razor-sharp teeth. When hungry, the piranha can be both bold and **savage**. But for such a frightening fish, it is not very big. Most are about the size of an adult's hand.

Some piranhas are silver in colour, with orange undersides. Others are almost totally black. All have blunt heads, saw-edged bellies, and strong jaws.

In the Amazon River, there are 20 different kinds of piranhas. The most famous is the red-bellied piranha. It has the strongest jaws and the sharpest teeth.

Why do you suppose that when water levels get low, piranhas hunt in larger schools than they would otherwise? (Hint: How much of your body can you fit underwater in the tub once you start letting the water out?)

Red-bellied piranha.
© Kevin Schafer/Corbis

When water levels are low, this piranha hunts in schools of more than 100 fish. Many schools join in the feast if a large animal has been attacked. But normally red-bellied piranhas prefer **prey** only slightly larger than themselves.

Usually a group of red-bellied piranhas swim around together in search of prey. The moment the prey is found, the fish signal each other. Piranhas have excellent hearing, so it's possible that they signal each other with sounds. Each fish in the group has a chance to take a bite and then swim away, making way for the others.

Most piranhas never kill large animals, and they almost never kill humans. The smell of blood attracts piranhas, but most of them feed on what is left by others rather than making fresh kills. For this reason their reputation for being ferocious is not deserved.

LEARN MORE! READ THESE ARTICLES…
AMAZON: A CLOSE LOOK AT RIVER LIFE (VOLUME 9)
FISH (VOLUME 11) • RIVERS (VOLUME 1)

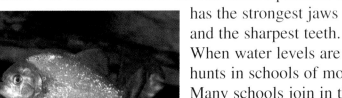

Groups of piranhas hide out and chase and attack fish that swim by.
© John Madere/Corbis

DID YOU KNOW?
The name 'piranha' comes from the Portuguese words for 'fish' and 'tooth'.

Answer: When river water levels are low, there's less room for fish to spread out, so piranhas have to hunt together in large groups.

Predators
of the Sea

When the first dinosaurs walked on Earth, sharks were already swimming in the sea. The dinosaurs are long gone, but sharks are still a force to be reckoned with.

Great white sharks, in particular, are feared as man-eaters. It's hard to fight them, because they are so strong and fast in the water. Their tough

(Top) Scalloped hammerhead shark; (bottom) swimming shark.

skin is protected by tiny toothlike scales. In their big mouths are rows and rows of sharp teeth that rip like the edge of a saw. Sharks continue to grow teeth all their lives. A great white can make a quick meal out of almost anything!

The hammerhead shark can also be dangerous. Don't be fooled by its awkward-looking rectangle of a head. In general, most shark attacks take place in shallow water, where sharks sometimes go to hunt for fish. A hungry shark can easily mistake a human arm or leg for a tasty fish.

Most kinds of sharks are not dangerous to people. This includes the largest shark of all, the whale shark. Whale sharks can be 15 metres long, but they feed on small fish and on tiny life forms called plankton. Other sharks eat fish of all sizes. The shark appears out of nowhere, often from below, to take its prey by surprise.

Did you know that a shark has to keep swimming all the time? Its body is made in such a way that if it doesn't swim, it will sink to the bottom of the sea. Good thing sharks know how to sleep while they swim!

LEARN MORE! READ THESE ARTICLES...
DEEP-SEA LIFE (VOLUME 11) • OCEANS (VOLUME 1)
WHALES (VOLUME 12)

SEARCH LIGHT

Find and correct the error in the following sentence: Hammerhead sharks got their name because they bash their prey over the head.

Scuba divers photograph a whale shark. Whale sharks usually swim slowly near the surface and have even been hit by ships.
© Jeffrey L. Rotman/Corbis

Answer: Hammerhead sharks got their name because their heads look like hammers.

43

There is an amazing variety of sea life on and around the Great Barrier Reef. There are about 400 types of hard coral, about 215 types of birds, and more than 1,500 types of fish, many with bright colours and unusual shapes.

DID YOU KNOW?
The Great Barrier Reef is the largest structure ever built by living things. It is longer than the Great Wall of China and much wider.

Builders in the Sea

Two parts of the animal are called coral. What are they?

A coral is a soft little sea animal that looks like a bit of jelly. It is no bigger than the end of your little finger. At one end it has a mouth surrounded by little arms called 'tentacles'. The tentacles gather food. When they touch a tiny plant or animal floating nearby, they pull these inside the mouth.

The baby coral swims through the water until it finds a place to build its house, and then it never swims again. Using special glue from inside its body, it sticks itself to a rock or to another piece of coral. Once it is stuck, it starts to build itself a house with a juice from its body that turns into a kind of stone. The hard little shell houses are called coral too.

© Royalty-Free/Corbis

(Top) Orange cup coral; (bottom) yellow and gray coral.

In the ocean where the water is warm, the coral grows in lovely ocean gardens. It grows in just about every colour and shape you can think of. It may grow to look like lace, a fan, a leaf, a brain, the horns of a deer, or a ribbon.

One day a bud will grow on the coral. This bud grows into a new coral animal. After many years there are so many coral houses built on top of one another and next to each other that they become a great wall called a 'reef'.

Sometimes coral may grow together to form a reef hundreds of kilometres long. The largest coral reef in the world is the Great Barrier Reef near Australia. It is more than 2,000 kilometres long.

LEARN MORE! READ THESE ARTICLES...
GREAT BARRIER REEF (VOLUME 7) • OCEANS (VOLUME 1)
THE GREAT WALL (VOLUME 7)

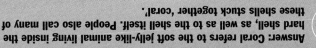

SEARCH LIGHT

Which of the following statements are true about sponges?
a) Sponges can be found mainly in the sea.
b) Sponges eat by straining the water around them.
c) The sponges in your house probably came from the sea.

Plants or Animals?

Sponges are strange animals. They don't have the body parts - inside or outside - that we expect an animal to have. They don't even move around. Instead, they stay attached to an underwater rock or coral reef, just like plants. For a long time, people thought sponges were plants. Scientists decided that sponges are animals only after watching them eating food by drawing it into their bodies.

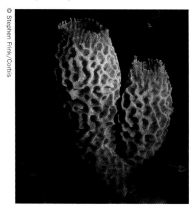

There are nearly 5,000 different kinds of sponges. Most live in the sea, but a few like freshwater. Sponges may be flat like spreading moss. Or they may look like trees with branching arms. Some are as tiny as a bean, while others are as tall as a person. Some are smooth and mushy, while others are rough, hard, and prickly. Some are dull and drab, while others are brightly coloured.

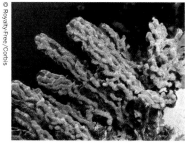

(Top) Vase sponge; (bottom) marine sponges.

A sponge gets oxygen to breathe and food particles to eat by straining water through its body. Sometimes fish, shrimp, and other creatures live inside a sponge. A few sponges attach themselves to crab shells and go wherever the crab goes.

People dive to collect sponges or pull them up with hooks. Afterward the sponges are dried, cleaned, and trimmed. The fleshy parts are thrown away, and only the 'spongy' skeleton is used. The ancient Greeks and Romans used sponges to pad their armour and helmets. People still use sponges for scrubbing themselves clean, for painting, and for making medicines. However, factory-made sponges have taken the place of natural sponges in most homes.

LEARN MORE! READ THESE ARTICLES...
CORAL (VOLUME 11) • MOLLUSCS (VOLUME 11) • OCEANS (VOLUME 1)

A school of fish swims near some sponges. A few animals eat sponges, but most leave them alone because of their unpleasant taste and smell.
© Royalty-Free/Corbis

Answer: a) Sponges can be found mainly in the sea.
b) Sponges eat by straining the water around them.

47

DID YOU KNOW?

Molluscs have been a popular food for thousands of years. Scientists have found old piles of shells, some over three metres tall, where ancient people threw the rubbish from their meals of clams and oysters.

Shell-Dwelling Animals

There are many different shelled animals. The smallest live in shells as tiny as the letter 'O'. The largest, such as the giant squids, weigh more than two tonnes! Some of these animals belong to a group called 'molluscs'. And you might be surprised to know that there are about 100,000 kinds of them!

Most molluscs - such as snails, clams, oysters, and mussels -

Snail on a child's hand.
© Lance Nelson/Corbis

have shells. But some, such as octopuses and squid, have little or none at all. And not all kinds of animals with shells are molluscs. Crabs and lobsters have shells, but they are not molluscs.

Although most molluscs live in the water, some are found on land. Snails live in forests and gardens.

Newborn molluscs are squishy and helpless. They need protection from enemies that would eat them. They get this protection from the shell they build around themselves. Shells are really one-room houses that molluscs build out of their own bodies. It's as easy for them to do this as it is for you to grow fingernails. Each shell has room for just one animal.

Molluscs eat tiny bits of food that float with the moving water. They also eat the **algae** that cover rocks. Part of this food is used to build their bodies. The rest helps them build their shells. A mollusc and its shell keep growing as long as the mollusc lives.

When a mollusc dies, it leaves behind its shell. That is why most of the shells you find on the beach are empty. Mollusc shells can last for thousands of years - a reminder of how long molluscs have been living on the Earth.

LEARN MORE! READ THESE ARTICLES...
GREAT BARRIER REEF (VOLUME 7) • OCEANS (VOLUME 1) • OCTOPUSES (VOLUME 11)

SEARCH LIGHT

Which of the following are molluscs?
- crabs
- snails
- prawns
- oysters
- squids

Mussels, pictured here in a tide pool, are a kind of mollusc. Mussels are found all over the world, mostly in cool seas.
© Kennan Ward/Corbis

Answer: Snails, oysters, and squid are all molluscs.

SEARCH LIGHT

What are two ways that an octopus can escape from an enemy?

Eight-Armed Wonders

People used to tell scary stories about a deep-sea monster that wrapped its many long arms around a ship and dragged it down to the bottom of the ocean. They called the monster a 'devilfish'.

Today we know that this wasn't a monster at all. It was an octopus - an animal with eight arms that lives in the ocean. Octopuses are members of an animal group called molluscs, which includes squid, clams, and oysters.

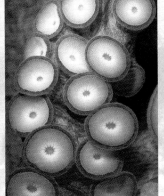

Suckers on the underside of the tentacle of a giant Pacific octopus.
© Stuart Westmorland/Corbis

There are nearly 50 kinds of octopus. Some are only a few centimetres long. The largest is longer than 9 metres and may weigh more than 68 kilos. But no octopus grows large enough to attack a ship!

An octopus usually lives alone amongst the rocks on the bottom of the ocean. Sometimes it moves rocks with its long arms, or **tentacles**, to make a little cave for itself. On the underside of each of its tentacles are many little round suckers, or **suction** cups. These help the octopus climb over rocks and hold on to things.

Octopuses like to eat shellfish such as crabs, lobsters, and mussels. An octopus will crawl about on its rubbery tentacles as it looks for food. But it can also swim very fast. An octopus sometimes hunts fish, chasing them until they are too tired to swim anymore. Then the octopus tightly wraps its arms around the fish and eats them.

But the octopus has enemies too. It usually tries to hide from them. Many octopuses can hide by changing colour to match the area around them. If that doesn't work, the octopus shoots black ink into the water around it. The cloudy water confuses the enemy and helps the octopus get away.

LEARN MORE! READ THESE ARTICLES…
DEEP-SEA LIFE (VOLUME 11) • MOLLUSCS (VOLUME 11)
OCEANS (VOLUME 1)

An octopus has eight arms, or tentacles. Its name comes from a Greek word that means 'eight-footed'.
© Stephen Frink/Corbis

DID YOU KNOW?
Octopuses are very smart. In fact, next to dolphins and whales, the common octopus is perhaps the smartest animal living in the ocean!

Answer: It can change colour and squirt ink into the water.

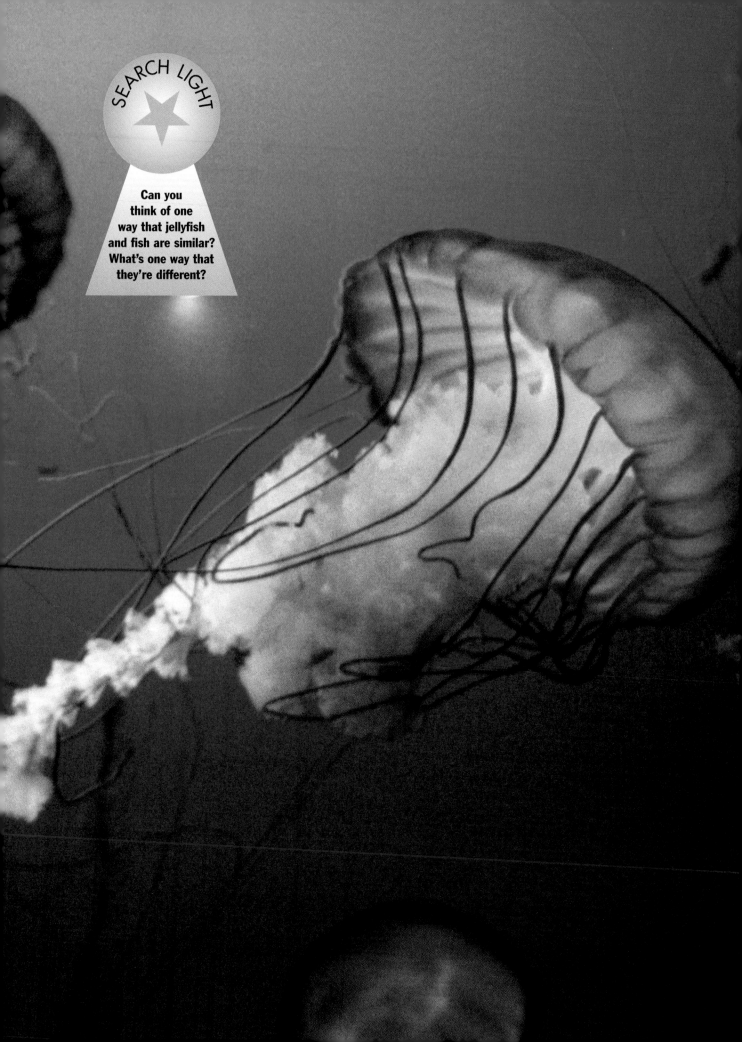

SEARCH LIGHT

Can you think of one way that jellyfish and fish are similar? What's one way that they're different?

Boneless Blobs
of the Sea

A jellyfish is not a fish at all. Unlike fish it has no bones, and most of its body is like jelly. It does not have a brain or a heart. What it does have is a set of **tentacles** that can sting its prey - or a person!

Jellyfish are related to corals and sea anemones. They can be found in all oceans. There are about 200 kinds of jellyfish, in different forms, sizes, and colours. Some jellyfish are barely large enough to be seen. Others can be more than two metres around. Jellyfish may be transparent or brown, pink, white, or blue. Some kinds glow in the dark sea.

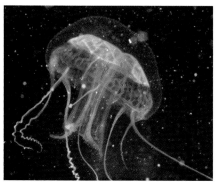

Jellyfish in dark waters.
© Jeffrey L. Rotman/Corbis

A jellyfish usually has the shape of an umbrella. It can have a few or many tentacles. Sometimes it has simple eyes around the edge of the 'umbrella'. The mouth and the stomach are in the middle of the 'umbrella'. The jellyfish has simple muscles on the underside that **contract** the body, much like the closing of an umbrella. This helps it swim.

Inside the tentacles of a jellyfish are poisonous stinging cells. These cells can stun small animals, which the jellyfish then pulls into its mouth. Some jellyfish feed on tiny animals and plants that their bodies catch as they drift through the water.

Some jellyfish can be very dangerous to humans. Even a small sting from the jellyfish called sea wasps can cause death within a few minutes. It's best just to look at jellyfish from a distance and not get too close.

LEARN MORE! READ THESE ARTICLES...
CORAL (VOLUME 11) • GREAT BARRIER REEF (VOLUME 7)
OCEANS (VOLUME 1)

Jellyfish sometimes sting swimmers who accidentally brush up against them in the water. Even dead jellyfish that have washed up on the beach can be dangerous and should not be touched.
© Danny Lehman/Corbis

Answer: The most obvious thing that jellyfish and fish share is their ocean home. One big difference between them is that jellyfish have no bones but fish do.

Flashing Lights!

It is very dark deep below the surface of the oceans of the world. This dark area is called the '**abyssal** zone'. It is a black, soundless place where the water is very still. This zone lies thousands of metres below the water's surface.

You wouldn't think it, but there are many kinds of living things to be found in the abyss. For a very long time, people believed that nothing could live down there because there isn't any light. But scientists who investigated the deep sea found plenty of life!

Many forms of life were discovered near cracks on the ocean floor. These are called 'rift communities'. The huge cracks, or fissures, are between two of the **plates** that make up the Earth's crust. These fissures are hot-water vents that raise the temperature of the water around them. The fissures are rich in **minerals**.

Deep-sea anglerfish.
© Bruce Robinson/Corbis

Deep-sea animals include certain kinds of squid, octopuses, worms, and fish. Because it is difficult to study animals at such levels, not much is known about their behaviour or surroundings. But it is known that deep-sea animals have special features that allow them to live in conditions in which other animals could not. These features are called **adaptations**.

Many deep-sea fish and other creatures flash with their own lights. This ability to give off light is called 'bioluminescence'. It is an adaptation for living in the darkness of the deep sea. Some deep-sea animals have coloured lights on different parts of the body. Their bodies keep flashing on and off. It is possible that the animals are speaking to each other with their lights.

LEARN MORE! READ THESE ARTICLES...
FISH (VOLUME 11) • OCEANS (VOLUME 1) • SUBMARINES (VOLUME 2)

Tube worms are just one example of the many types of life found deep in the ocean. Tube worms are large red worms that live inside white tubes that are attached to the ocean floor.
© F. Grassle, Woods Hole Oceanographic Institution

Answer: The deepest part of the ocean is called the abyssal zone.

The World's Largest Population

The Earth is home to more insects than any other kind of animal. Insects are unique among all creatures because their bodies are divided into three parts - the head, the thorax, and the abdomen. The head contains the mouth, the eyes, and the **antennas**. Some insects use their antennas for smelling. The thorax is similar to a person's chest. If an insect has wings, they are attached to the thorax. And some insects have ears on the thorax. The abdomen contains a large part of the **digestive system**.

Instead of having bones, insects have an outer covering to support the body. The muscles are attached to this covering. The outer layer of the covering is waxy and **waterproof**.

All insects have six legs. Their legs, like their wings, are attached to the thorax. Each leg has five different bending places. It's like having five knees.

Each kind of insect has features that help it get along in the world. The pond skater has little cups on its feet so that it can walk on water. Dragonflies can hover and turn in the air like little helicopters. They even look like helicopters!

Some insects make sounds like music. Perhaps the most beautiful music is made by the snowy tree cricket. This insect uses one of its front wings as a fiddle and the other as a bow. Locusts have two tiny shell-like drums close to their wings. When the wings flap, these drums sound like fingers tapping on a metal lid. Grasshoppers make sounds by rubbing their wings or their back legs together. In some places people keep crickets or grasshoppers in cages to listen to their songs.

LEARN MORE! READ THESE ARTICLES...
AMPHIBIANS (VOLUME 11) • MAMMALS (VOLUME 12)
REPTILES (VOLUME 11)

DID YOU KNOW?
It may seem hard to believe, but in the countryside almost all the noises you hear at night are made by insects and frogs - even the ones that sound like birds or people.

SEARCH LIGHT

What
are the
three parts of
an insect's body?

Answer: The three parts of an insect's body are the head, the thorax, and the abdomen.

Two leafcutting ants are hard at work clipping out pieces of a leaf in a rainforest in Costa Rica. The fragments are transported to an underground nest that can include over 1,000 chambers and house millions of individual ants. The ants physically and chemically create 'gardens' of fungus that grow on the chewed leaves. The fungus then provides them with food.
© Steve Kaufman/Corbis

Insect Castle Builders

Most ants live in nests that they build in protected places. Many live underground, sometimes under a rock. Some ants live in trees or inside wild plants. Others build their nests on the ground, using tiny sticks, sand, mud, gravel, and even leaves.

Large ant hill in the Northern Territory of Australia.
© Penny Tweedie/Corbis

An ant hill is a mound of sand or dirt where thousands of ants live and work. Inside the hill are special rooms where food is kept and other rooms for baby ants. Tunnels connect the rooms. Worker ants build the nest, make tunnels, and repair any damage to the ant hill.

Soldier ants guard the ant hill day and night and protect it from enemies. An ant has long feelers, called antennas, that stick out from its head. It can give messages to other ants by tapping them with its antennas. Ants smell with their antennas too. They use scents to tell whether another ant is a friend or an enemy. If an ant from another nest wanders into the ant hill, the soldiers will attack it. Deadly wars are often fought between two nests of ants.

The whole nest is ruled by the queen ant, the mother of all the ants. The queen lays her eggs in a special room in the ant hill, while the other ants feed, clean, and protect her.

The 'ant castle' doesn't have a barn or a stable. But in one room certain kinds of ants keep aphids, which are tiny green insects. Aphids are called 'ant cows' because the ants 'milk' them to get a sweet juice the aphids produce. Other ants are like farmers too. They grow fungus inside their nests, and the fungus is all they eat!

SEARCH LIGHT

Why do you think ants touch feelers whenever they meet? (Hint: What important function do the feelers, or antennas, serve?)

LEARN MORE! READ THESE ARTICLES...
CARNIVOROUS PLANTS (VOLUME 10) • INSECTS (VOLUME 11) • SAND (VOLUME 1)

Answer: Ants touch when they meet because that's how they communicate with one another. They also use their feelers to tell if an ant is an enemy or a friend.

SEARCH LIGHT

★

True
or false?
Drones
have stingers.

Inside the Hive

Inside a honeybee hive you'll see bees. But you'll also see hundreds of little six-sided rooms, or 'cells'. The bees build these cells with a wax - beeswax - that they make inside their bodies.

The bees store many things in the wax cells, including honey, **nectar**, and a food called 'bee bread'. Bee bread is made of flower **pollen** mixed with honey. The cells are also used to hold the tiny eggs that will hatch into baby bees.

A bee pollinates a flower.
© George D. Lepp/Corbis

Most of the bees' work is done in spring and summer. That's when the honey is made and stored and when the queen bee lays most of her eggs. The queen bee is the biggest bee in the hive.

There are two other kinds of bee in the hive: drones and workers. Drones are larger than the workers and have no stingers. They don't do any work, but one drone mates with the queen and is the father of all the hive's workers.

Each of the worker bees has a special job. Some build the cells in the hive, and others keep the hive clean. Some workers are soldiers that guard the hive and chase away any bees, wasps, and other insects that might try to steal the hive's honey.

Other worker bees fly out to visit flowers and blossoms. They take pollen and nectar back to the hive to make bee bread and honey. Some bees even stay by the door of the hive and flap their wings quickly to blow cool air through the hive.

DID YOU KNOW?
Bees can tell if an intruder has entered the hive because the intruder smells different. But one kind of moth has found a way to sneak into hives. It fakes the smell of the hive just long enough to get in and steal some honey.

LEARN MORE! READ THESE ARTICLES...
BATS (VOLUME 12) • HONEYSUCKLE (VOLUME 10) • INSECTS (VOLUME 11)

Bees go about their work on a man-made honeycomb.
© Lynda Richardson/Corbis

Answer: FALSE. Only worker bees and queens have stingers.

Fly by Day, Fly by Night

Butterflies and moths are found throughout the world, from deserts to hot jungles to high up in snowy mountains. You can see them on every continent except Antarctica.

Butterflies and moths are insects, and like all insects they have three pairs of legs. Their bodies are divided into three sections: head, **thorax**,

Brown moth.
© Karen Tweedy-Holmes/Corbis

and **abdomen**. On either side of the head is a large special eye. These eyes are able to detect the smallest movement. But they cannot see faraway things very clearly.

The thorax, the middle section of the body, has two pairs of wings. The wings in front are usually larger. Dust-like scales cover the wings, body, and legs. If you happen to touch a butterfly or moth, these scales will come off in your hand.

If you want to know whether you are looking at a butterfly or a moth, you should look at its **antennae**. Butterflies and moths use their antennae to hear and smell. Butterfly antennae end in little round knobs. Moth antennae may look like tiny feathers or threads.

The most striking thing about butterflies is their colouring. Most are bright and beautiful. But most moths are dull coloured, with thicker bodies and smaller wings. Butterflies hold their wings straight up over their backs when they rest. Moths rest with their wings spread out. Butterflies are active during the day. But moths usually fly around at night.

Many butterflies and moths seem to like sweet things. **Nectar** from flowers is an important part of their diet. Some will eat mosses and ferns. Others like cones, fruits, and seeds, but some do not eat at all and live for only a short time!

LEARN MORE! READ THESE ARTICLES...
BATS (VOLUME 12) • HONEYSUCKLE (VOLUME 10)
INSECTS (VOLUME 11)

SEARCH LIGHT

When do most butterflies fly, during the day or at night?

A cracker butterfly rests on the leaf of a plant.
© George D. Lepp/Corbis

Cockroaches usually run and hide when a light is turned on in a dark room.

Indestructible Insects

True or false? Most cockroaches hide at night and come out during the day.

Cockroaches have been around for many millions of years. This means that cockroaches lived through times when many other animals disappeared forever. They are very tough insects indeed. One type, the Oriental cockroach, can live for a month without food!

Cockroaches are found nearly everywhere. Some kinds live outside, but others live indoors alongside humans. These kinds are pests. They like warm dark areas in homes, offices, ships, trains, and even airplanes. Their broad flat bodies can squeeze through the narrowest of cracks. Although cockroaches may look like beetles, they are related to crickets. Like them, cockroaches use their long **antennae** on their heads for feeling through dark places.

Cockroaches usually hide during the day and come out at night to feed. They eat all sorts of plant and animal products, including paper, clothing, books, and other insects. Some cockroaches even eat other cockroaches.

Their feeding causes a lot of damage. And they have a nasty smell too. They can also cause allergies and are thought to spread diseases to humans. No wonder cockroaches are considered among the worst household pests.

Humans get rid of cockroaches with common poisons and traps. But cockroaches have many other enemies besides humans. Spiders, frogs, toads, lizards, and birds all feed on them.

There are more than 3,500 types of cockroach. Some are small, while others reach lengths of seven centimetres. Many are colourful. Most have two pairs of wings. Some, such as the American cockroach, can fly long distances. Others, such as the Oriental cockroach, can't fly at all. But all cockroaches have long powerful legs and can run very fast.

LEARN MORE! READ THESE ARTICLES…

DID YOU KNOW?
Many scientists believe that the cockroach is one of the few animals that could survive a nuclear bomb blast.

Answer: FALSE. Cockroaches usually hide during the day and come out at night to feed.

65

True
or false?
Some crickets
can fly.

**There are a number of myths about crickets. Some people
believe that harming a cricket will lead to bad luck.**

© Cordaiy Photo Library Ltd./Corbis

The Wing Singers

A cricket never opens its mouth to chirp. Instead, it raises its stiff leathery front wings and rubs one over the other to make its high creaking sound. It's a loud noise for such a tiny insect. Some crickets are as small as your thumbnail.

Cricket on the head of a flower.
© Dennis Johnson—Papilio/Corbis

Only male crickets have music-making wings. The chirping lets female crickets know where to find them, and it also keeps other male crickets away. The smooth wings of female crickets make no sound. Some kinds of male and female crickets use their back wings for flying. But most crickets travel by hopping and jumping.

Some crickets eat only tiny insects. Others will eat almost anything. Crickets have such strong jaws that they can bite through clothes and even leather.

Like other insects, a cricket has six legs. On its feet there are tiny claws that help it dig or run along on a tree limb or ceiling. You'll never guess where a cricket's ears are. They're down near the joints of its front legs!

There are many different kinds of cricket. Crickets are black, green-brown, whitish, and straw coloured. There are the field crickets and brown house crickets. Both chirp during the day and night. But the white and green tree crickets and the bush crickets chirp only at night.

A special kind of cricket in North America is called a 'thermometer cricket'. Try counting how many times it chirps in 15 seconds and add 40 to it. Now you know the temperature in Fahrenheit degrees! The crickets chirp faster as the weather gets warmer.

DID YOU KNOW?

Crickets are known to be such good 'singers' that they were once commonly kept in Chinese houses as pets.

LEARN MORE! READ THESE ARTICLES…
GRASSHOPPERS (VOLUME 11) • INSECTS (VOLUME 11) • TEMPERATURES (VOLUME 2)

Grasshoppers are green, olive, or brown and
may have yellow or red markings.
© Karl Switak—Gallo Images/Corbis

68

Garden-Variety Hoppers

Grasshoppers are insects that are found all over the world. They live in all kinds of places but are most common in grasslands and tropical forests. One type spends most of its life on floating plants. But grasshoppers also live in people's gardens. Their brown or green colouring helps them blend in with the plants and soil around them.

Bladder grasshopper.
© Anthony Bannister—Gallo Images/Corbis

The reason grasshoppers are fond of gardens is that they are **vegetarians**. And people grow many things that grasshoppers like to eat. In some parts of the world, grasshoppers called locusts travel in huge swarms that can destroy a whole season's worth of crops.

The grasshopper itself has to be careful as well. Some if its relatives, such as the mantises, will make a meal out of a grasshopper. Many birds, frogs, and snakes also eat any grasshopper they find. In certain parts of the world, even people eat grasshoppers. Whether they are dried, fried, jellied, roasted, dipped in honey, or ground into **meal**, they can be a good source of **nutrients**.

But grasshoppers have their ways of avoiding danger too. They can smell and hear an enemy, and, of course, they can hop. A grasshopper can hop so well because of its long hind legs. And though grasshoppers usually hop or crawl to get around, most kinds can also fly.

Usually, male grasshoppers are the ones that chirp or sing. They rub their wings together, or they rub their hind legs against their front wings. The song is the male's way of calling the female grasshopper.

LEARN MORE! READ THESE ARTICLES…
CRICKETS (VOLUME 11) • KANGAROOS (VOLUME 12) • WHEAT (VOLUME 10)

Answer: Farmers don't like locusts because they destroy crops.

An Itchy Situation

SEARCH LIGHT

Find and correct the errors in the following sentence: Mosquitoes live in dry places such as deserts, because they must lay their eggs in sand.

'M-m-m-m-m-m-s-s-z-z-sz-sz-n-n-z-z-zing-ing-ing!'

The humming sound you hear when a mosquito is near your ear comes from the fast beat of the mosquito's wings. Actually, that's the hum of the female mosquito. It is only the female mosquito that bites and leaves those itchy lumps on your arms or legs. The male mosquito seems to be satisfied with a meal of nectar and other plant juices.

Mosquitoes are insects that are usually found wherever the weather is damp or where there are rivers, lakes, or swamps. That's because mosquitoes must lay their eggs in water. Otherwise, the eggs could not hatch. Mosquitoes sometimes lay their eggs in ponds, and other times they lay them in ditches. They will even lay them in tins partly filled with rainwater. When the eggs hatch, the young mosquitoes look like little worms.

Sometimes mosquitoes fly so high up in the air that they even get in through the open windows of tall apartment buildings in big cities. In the far north, near the North Pole, there are so many mosquitoes in summer that when they fly they look like black clouds.

Magnified image of young, newly hatched mosquitoes.
© Science Pictures Limited/Corbis

Getting rid of mosquitoes is difficult. One way is to drain all the water out of ditches, swamps, and ponds where they lay their eggs. To destroy full-grown mosquitoes, different kinds of insecticides are used. An insecticide is a powder or liquid for killing harmful insects. Unfortunately, it can be dangerous for animals and people too.

LEARN MORE! READ THESE ARTICLES…
BEES (VOLUME 11) • INSECTS (VOLUME 11) • SWAMPS (VOLUME 1)

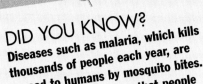

A female mosquito sucks blood from a human arm.

Answer: Mosquitoes live in damp places or near rivers, swamps, and lakes, because they must lay their eggs in water.

71

The Silk Spinners

SEARCH LIGHT

How does the pirate spider catch its food?

Spiders belong to a large group of animals called 'arthropods'. This group also includes crabs, centipedes, and insects. Arthropods have their skeletons on the outside of their bodies.

Though they're part of the same larger group, spiders are not insects. Insects have six legs, while spiders have eight. This makes them part of a smaller group, the arachnids. Arachnids - including **scorpions** and ticks - have eight walking legs. Many spiders and other arachnids use **venom** to kill their prey.

Spiders also spin silk. In fact, the word 'spider' comes from an old English word that means 'to spin'. Spiders have silk-making organs called 'spinnerets' near the back of their bodies. They spin silk from a liquid made by special **glands**. It becomes solid thread after the spider pushes it out of its body.

Spiders spin different types of silk for different uses. Some silk is stronger than steel wire. Spiders use silk for webs to trap food, for lining

Jumping spider ready to pounce.
© Robert Pickett/Corbis

their nests, and to hold the eggs they lay. When a spider has to escape from an enemy, it may quickly spin a getaway thread and drop out of sight on it.

Not all spiders catch food in a web. Some, such as the jumping spider, pounce like a cat to capture insects. Others spin silk funnels, where they hide during the day before going hunting at night. The brightly coloured crab spider hides between flower petals and grabs insects looking for nectar. Pirate spiders creep inside the webs spun by other spiders and then eat them up.

LEARN MORE! READ THESE ARTICLES...
AMAZON: A CLOSE LOOK AT RIVER LIFE (VOLUME 9) • INSECTS (VOLUME 11)
A STORY FROM GHANA: ANANSE AND THE WISDOM POT (VOLUME 5)

Many spiders spin webs to trap food - most often insects such as this unfortunate butterfly.
© Tecmap Corporation—Eric Curry/Corbis

DID YOU KNOW?

Spiders live everywhere, even underwater. Water spiders are called 'diving bells' because they build bell-shaped webs underwater. The bell webs trap air bubbles for the spider to breathe.

Answer: A pirate spider eats other spiders out of their own webs.

Snakes, Lizards, and Other Dry-Scaled Beasts

Long before there were any birds, and long before mammals, there were reptiles. In fact, scientists believe that the first reptiles appeared on Earth more than 300 million years ago. The reptiles that exist today include snakes, lizards, turtles, crocodiles, and alligators. Snakes and lizards account for the greatest number of reptiles. Altogether there are more than 5,500 different kinds of snakes and lizards.

SEARCH LIGHT

Which came first, birds, mammals, or reptiles?

Unlike other animals with backbones, reptiles have dry scales covering their bodies. These scales are replaced throughout a reptile's lifetime. Snakes shed all of their scales at once. Lizards, crocodiles, and turtles shed their scales bit by bit.

DID YOU KNOW?
No modern reptile can truly fly, but some snakes and lizards can flatten their bodies and glide from tall trees.

Birds and mammals **evolved** from reptiles millions of years ago. But while birds and mammals are warm-blooded, meaning that their temperature stays the same all the time, a reptile's body temperature is changed by the surrounding area's temperature. Because of this, reptiles are said to be 'cold-blooded'. They warm or cool themselves by moving to warmer or cooler locations. Most reptiles **hibernate** during the winter.

Today's reptiles come in many sizes. Some tiny lizards are less than 5 centimetres long. Anacondas, the world's largest snakes, grow to more than 9 metres long. The largest of the lizards is the Komodo dragon, which can reach more than 3 metres long. And the leatherback sea turtle can be more than 3 metres long and weigh more than 680 kilos.

One of the most fascinating aspects of reptiles is how long many of them can live. Many kinds of reptiles have lived for more than 20 years in zoos. And some types of turtle have been known to live for more than 150 years!

LEARN MORE! READ THESE ARTICLES…
BIRDS (VOLUME 11) • CHARLES DARWIN (VOLUME 4) • MAMMALS (VOLUME 12)

SEARCH LIGHT

True or false? Alligator is another name for a crocodile.

Today, many alligators and crocodiles are in danger of becoming extinct. One reason is that many are killed each year for sport or for their skins, which are used to make purses, shoes, and belts. These crocodiles are lying in the grass near Moramanga, Madagascar.
© Wolfgang Kaehler/Corbis

Modern Dinosaurs

If you're looking for reptiles that have been around since the days of the dinosaurs, try alligators and crocodiles. These large lizard-like animals are related to the giant reptiles of the past.

Alligators and crocodiles are closely related. They look a lot alike, but alligators have a broad flat head with a rounded **snout**. Most crocodiles have

Alligators in the Okefenokee Swamp, Georgia, U.S.
© David Muench/Corbis

a narrow, pointed snout. When a crocodile closes its mouth, the fourth tooth on each side of its lower jaw sticks out. Crocodiles are larger than alligators. They range from 2 to more than 6 metres long, while most alligators are about 1.8 to 2.4 metres long.

Alligators and most crocodiles live along the edges of large bodies of freshwater such as lakes, swamps, and rivers. They spend a lot of time in the water, but they can also be found on land near the water. Large adults can stay under water for over an hour without breathing.

Both animals have long snouts, powerful tails, and thick skin with bony plates underneath. Their eyes, ears, and nostrils are located on top of their long heads. Alligators and crocodiles often float with only their eyes and noses showing.

Crocodiles can be found in **tropical** swamps and rivers in Asia, Australia, Africa, and South America. Alligators are less widespread. The American alligator lives in the south-eastern United States. In South America there are various alligators called caimans. The Chinese alligator lives in the Yangtze River and is smaller than the American alligator.

Adult alligators and crocodiles eat mostly fish, small mammals, and birds. Sometimes they may kill deer or cattle. Crocodiles are more likely than alligators to attack humans, though alligators will attack if cornered.

DID YOU KNOW?

There are saltwater crocodiles living in northern Australia and Southeast Asia. Australians call their crocodiles 'salties'.

LEARN MORE! READ THESE ARTICLES…
AMAZON: A CLOSE LOOK AT RIVER LIFE (VOLUME 9)
DINOSAURS: GIANTS OF THE PAST (VOLUME 1) • REPTILES (VOLUME 11)

Answer: FALSE. Though they are related, alligators and crocodiles are two different animals.

Legless Wonders

(Top) Ghost corn snake; (bottom) woma python.

Aside from worms, almost every animal you see on land has legs. But snakes are different. They don't have legs, or arms either. Most snakes move around by pushing against the ground, scraping it with their tough scales.

Snakes look slippery and slimy, but they're not. Their skin actually feels like cool soft leather. As a snake gets bigger, its skin gets tighter and tighter until the snake wiggles right out of it, wearing a new skin. A snake sheds its skin this way a few times a year.

The smallest snakes are no larger than worms. All snakes are hunters, though. Small snakes eat insects. Larger snakes eat rats or squirrels or rabbits. The huge pythons and anacondas can swallow a deer.

Some snakes use poison called 'venom' to catch animals. They deliver their poison with a bite. Others are constrictors, which means that they wrap themselves around their prey and suffocate it. Still other snakes eat bird eggs. Snakes swallow their food whole, without chewing. The jaws may be hinged so that the snake can eat something larger than its own head. A snake that has just eaten may not need another meal for days and days.

Snakes are eaten by big birds such as eagles, hawks, and owls. The Indian mongoose (a mammal) kills cobras. Wild hogs stamp on snakes to kill them. And, of course, many people kill snakes on sight.

Most snakes avoid people and won't hurt you if you don't bother them. Still, it's a good idea to leave wild snakes alone.

SEARCH LIGHT

True or false? Snakes chew their food.

LEARN MORE! READ THESE ARTICLES...
ANACONDAS (VOLUME 11) • KING COBRAS (VOLUME 11) • MONGOOSES (VOLUME 12)

The sea snake has a flat tail that it can use like an oar to move itself through the water.
© Brandon D. Cole/Corbis

Answer: FALSE. Snakes swallow their food whole.

SEARCH LIGHT

Find and correct the error in the following sentence: Anacondas kill their prey with a poisonous bite.

A Tight Squeeze

The giant anaconda is one of the longest and heaviest snakes in the world. But this South American animal is not poisonous. The anaconda kills its prey by squeezing it so hard that it cannot breathe.

The anaconda spends most of its time in water. When an animal goes to a river to drink, the anaconda grabs it. If the prey is large, the snake

Giant anaconda.
© Z. Leszczynski/Animals Animals

wraps itself around the animal and can choke it. The anaconda then drags the body into the water to keep it away from jaguars and biting ants that would be attracted to the **carcass**. When an anaconda eats a large animal, it gets so stuffed that it lies still for weeks to digest its meal!

There are two types of anaconda. The yellow anaconda is the smaller of the two. It is tan or greenish yellow with large black markings across its back and black blotches along its sides. Yellow anacondas are found in the southern Amazon River area. The giant anaconda is twice as big as the yellow anaconda. It's olive green with black spots. The giant anaconda lives in the South American tropics east of the Andes Mountains and on the Caribbean island of Trinidad. Giant anacondas can measure over 10 metres long.

Despite its size, a giant anaconda is not really violent. Scientists can simply pick up an anaconda and carry it off. But it may take several of them to lift the snake, especially if it just ate!

LEARN MORE! READ THESE ARTICLES…
AMAZON: A CLOSE LOOK AT RIVER LIFE (VOLUME 9)
REPTILES (VOLUME 11) • SNAKES (VOLUME 11)

A yellow anaconda lies on a log at the edge of the water. Although the anaconda spends much of its time in water, it may also crawl on land and even climb into trees to catch birds.
© Joe McDonald/Corbis

DID YOU KNOW?
Like most snakes, anacondas swallow their food whole. They can open their mouths wide enough to fit around an entire goat.

Reptile Royalty

The king cobra is the world's largest poisonous snake. It may grow to twice the length of a Ping-Pong table. Its **venom** is so powerful that elephants have died within three hours of a bite on the toe or trunk.

King cobras are olive-yellow to brownish black, sometimes with lighter bands across the back. Like other cobras, the king cobra is known for its unique 'threat display'. When it is angered or disturbed, it raises its head and **flares** its narrow, unmarked hood. This shows its yellow or red throat, which often is striped.

The king cobra can raise its head to a third of its entire length and may even move forward while upright. It is very curious by nature and often sits upright to see farther. It may be the most intelligent of all snakes.

The king cobra hunts in forests, fields, and villages. It usually eats other snakes and normally does not bite people. In **captivity** it is aggressive to strangers but recognizes its keeper and knows when it's mealtime. However, it can become dangerous during the mating season or when cornered or startled.

The female cobra builds a nest for laying eggs. Using a loop of her body as an arm, she pulls leaves, soil, and ground litter into a mound. In this nest she lays 20 to 40 eggs. She coils above or near the eggs for about two months and fiercely defends them.

The king cobra is found in parts of Asia from southern China to the Philippines, Indonesia, and India.

LEARN MORE! READ THESE ARTICLES...
INDIA (VOLUME 7) • REPTILES (VOLUME 11)
SNAKES (VOLUME 11)

SEARCH LIGHT

People are afraid of cobras and as a result often kill the snakes. Why do you think people are scared of cobras? (Hint: What would you worry about if you came face to face with a cobra?)

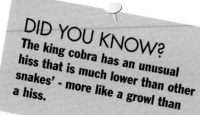

DID YOU KNOW?
The king cobra has an unusual hiss that is much lower than other snakes' - more like a growl than a hiss.

The king cobra (like other cobras) performs the famous 'threat display' by pulling the ribs of the neck sideways and forward. This flattens the neck into a hood.
© E. Hanumantha Rao/NHPA

Answer: Because cobras are poisonous and have occasionally killed people with their bite, many consider the snake a danger to humans. Cobras also have a flaring 'hood' that makes them look threatening. Actually, far more snakes are injured and killed by people each year than the other way around.

Cousins of the Dinosaurs

When scientists first found remains of dinosaurs, they thought they had found giant lizards. They later realized that dinosaurs and lizards are different types of animals, but they are related. Both are types of reptiles.

(Top) Komodo dragon; (bottom) gecko.

There are many kinds of lizard. They may be green, grey, red, brown, blue, yellow, black, or almost any colour! Some are longer than a man, and some are so tiny you could hold them between your fingers. The smallest lizards in the world belong to the skink and gecko families. The largest is the Komodo dragon of Southeast Asia.

Most lizards have a long tail, dry scaly skin, strong short legs, and long toes. They also have sharp claws. Some have spiny scales under their toes, which help them cling to rocks or branches.

Draco lizards are also called the 'flying lizards'. They can't fly the way a bird does, but they have a tough skin that can spread out. They can jump from a tree and sail a long way through the air.

A little lizard called the 'American chameleon' is pretty and friendly. These tiny creatures are helpful to humans because they eat harmful insects. They seem to be able to change colour when they want to. They can't really do that, but their skins do change from brown to green when there are changes in light and temperature.

The Gila monster is one of the few lizards that are dangerous. It is black and pink or orange, which makes it easy to see. And that's a good thing because the Gila has a poisonous bite.

SEARCH LIGHT

True or false? The flying lizard doesn't really fly.

LEARN MORE! READ THESE ARTICLES...
CHAMELEONS (VOLUME 11) • DINOSAURS: GIANTS OF THE PAST (VOLUME 1)
REPTILES (VOLUME 11)

DID YOU KNOW?
If another animal tries to eat the glass lizard by grabbing its tail, the tail comes off. The other animal may then think it has caught the whole lizard.

The five-lined skink is very small. It usually grows to be only about 13 to 20 centimetres long.

Answer: TRUE. It jumps and glides through the air.

SEARCH LIGHT

What's wrong with the following statement: Chameleons can make their skin colour change in order to match their surroundings.

The Colour-Wizard Lizards

Many people believe that the lizard known as the 'chameleon' can make its colour change to match its surroundings. It's true that the colour of a chameleon's skin can change, but not as a result of the chameleon's decision. The colour change may help the chameleon avoid its enemies. The colour change is a form of **camouflage**, a disguise that lets something blend in with its surroundings.

Chameleon skin contains colour-causing substances called

Chameleon of South Africa.
© Erice Reisinger–Gallo Images/Corbis

'pigments' that change under certain conditions. For instance, on a day when there is no bright sunlight, chameleons appear grey or green. Bright sunlight causes the skin to darken. On cool nights the colour fades to a creamy colour. The skin also changes colour when chameleons are excited, angry, or afraid.

There are many types of chameleon. About half are found only on the African island nation of Madagascar. The others are found mostly south of Africa's Sahara desert, with another few in western Asia and southern Europe. The 'false chameleon', or anole, is often sold in pet stores. This lizard of the Americas changes colour, but not as dramatically as a true chameleon.

Chameleons live in trees, where they usually eat insects. They catch their prey with the help of their long and slender tongue. They shoot the tongue out, grab the prey on the sticky end, and then draw the tongue back into their mouth. Very large chameleons may even use their sticky tongues to catch birds.

Another unusual thing about chameleons is that each eye can move independently of the other, so they can see in different directions at once. This makes it very hard to sneak up on a chameleon.

LEARN MORE! READ THESE ARTICLES…
AFRICA (VOLUME 8) • LIZARDS (VOLUME 11) • MADAGASCAR (VOLUME 8)

The Parson's chameleon, from Madagascar, is one of the largest of its family.
© Royalty-Free/Corbis

> ## DID YOU KNOW?
>
> Some say that the chameleon's eyes helped inspire the invention of the military turret, a revolving tower. You can see turrets today on the tops of tanks.

Answer: Chameleons' skin colour does change. But they don't decide to change it, and it doesn't always change in order to match their surroundings.

Taking Their Time

Turtles are known as slow-moving animals. They were around during the age of dinosaurs more than 100 million years ago. Dinosaurs are gone now, but turtles are still here. Slow but steady wins the race!

Like the dinosaurs, turtles are reptiles. There are nearly 250 kinds of turtle in the world today. All turtles breathe air at least part of the time,

Three painted turtles perched on a rock.
© William Manning/Corbis

even sea turtles, which spend almost their whole life in the ocean. In addition to the ocean, turtles can live in ponds, lakes, or rivers. Other turtles live in forests or even hot desert sands, far away from water. Some people refer to land turtles as 'tortoises'.

Turtles come in all sizes. Some are no more than 10 centimetres long. At the other end of the scale, the Atlantic leatherback turtle may weigh as much as 680 kilos.

Even sea turtles go ashore to lay their eggs. The newly hatched baby turtles are completely on their own. They scramble from their nest under the sand and walk on their tiny new flippers to the water.

Land and sea turtles can take care of themselves because they carry their houses with them wherever they go. Their houses are their shells. Some turtles can close their shells completely. The snapping turtle can't, but it has a powerful bite for protection.

No matter where they live, turtles don't need to hunt for food or water all the time. Some have a special place inside their bodies where they can store water. And they can store food in the form of fat. Turtles can live for days or even weeks without having anything to eat or drink.

SEARCH LIGHT

Fill in the gap: Land turtles are sometimes called _____.

LEARN MORE! READ THESE ARTICLES…
AMPHIBIANS (VOLUME 11) • DINOSAURS: GIANTS OF THE PAST (VOLUME 1)
REPTILES (VOLUME 11)

DID YOU KNOW?
Turtles can live longer than people can. Turtles are known to have lived 150 years in the wild, and there are reports of turtles that were even older than that.

A boy kneels to investigate a small turtle. Turtles are found in lakes, ponds, salt marshes, rivers, forests, and even deserts.
© Ariel Skelley/Corbis

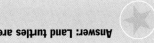

Answer: Land turtles are sometimes called tortoises.

DID YOU KNOW?
Salamanders were once believed to live in fire. The word 'salamander' comes from ancient words that mean 'fire lizard'.

SEARCH LIGHT

What's so special about amphibians? (Hint: Remember those Greek words.)

The Land-and-Water Dwellers

Millions of years ago, a group of fish began to breathe both in and out of the water. Eventually these fish made their way onto land and began to develop legs. These animals became amphibians, the ancestors of frogs, toads, and salamanders.

The word 'amphibian' comes from the Greek words *amphi*, which means 'both', and *bios*, which means 'life'. As their name suggests, amphibians live both in freshwater and on land.

Amphibians are cold-blooded animals. This means that an amphibian's body temperature generally matches the temperature around it. To warm up, amphibians often **bask** in the sun, and to cool off, they move into the shade. Amphibians must also stay near water. If their skin dries out, they will die.

There are three main groups of amphibian. The largest group includes the true frogs, tree frogs, and toads. True frogs have long hind legs and can swim and leap very well. Tree frogs have suction pads on their fingers and toes and can hold on to smooth surfaces. Toads have shorter legs than frogs, and their skin has a warty appearance.

The second group of amphibians is the salamanders, which have tails. The giant salamander of Japan and China is the largest of all amphibians. It can grow to a length of more than 1.5 metres.

The third group is the caecilians. These odd amphibians are rarely seen. They have long slender bodies with no arms or legs. They are also blind. A long flexible structure called a 'tentacle' sticks out next to each of their useless eyes. They use these tentacles to feel and sniff their way around.

LEARN MORE! READ THESE ARTICLES…

FROGS (VOLUME 11) • MARSHES (VOLUME 1) • RIVERS (VOLUME 1)

Answer: Amphibians are one of the few groups of animals that can live comfortably both in the water and on the land.

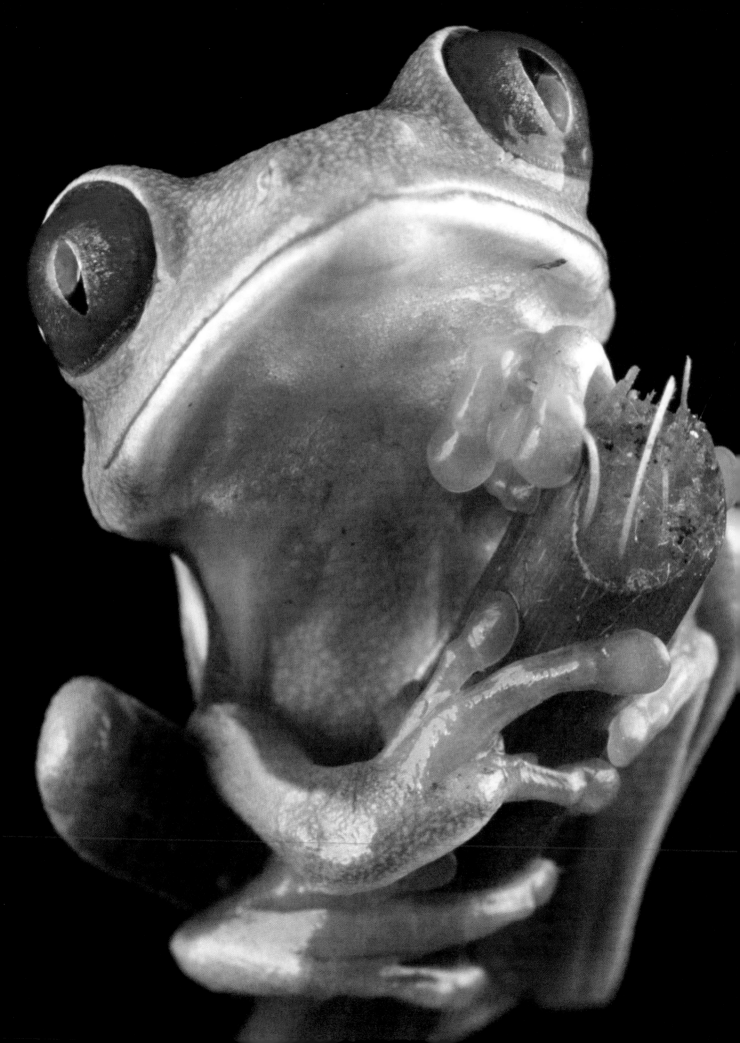

Amazing Changing Amphibians

Frogs are amphibians. This means they can live both in water and on land. And they have a life cycle that takes place in both environments.

A mother frog lays her eggs in the water. In a few days tiny tadpoles, or polliwogs, wriggle out of the eggs. The tadpoles don't look like frogs at all. They have long tails for swimming and slits called **gills** for breathing.

As a tadpole grows into a frog, it changes in many ways. Its tail gets shorter and shorter until it disappears. At the same time, the frog grows front and hind legs. The hind feet have long toes with webs between them to help in swimming and leaping. Plus, the gills disappear and **lungs** develop. Once these changes are complete, the creature is ready to live on land as well as in the water. It's now a frog. For some kinds of frogs, this process of change takes just two months. For others, it may take as long as three years.

Red-eyed leaf frog tadpoles.
© Michael & Patricia Fogden/Corbis

A frog has smooth moist skin. Its eyes are so big that they seem about to pop out of its head. These eyes help it find food. Its hind legs are more than twice as long as its front ones. The frog travels in great leaps on these long strong legs.

Frogs are closely related to toads. What's the difference between a frog and a toad? Well, a toad's skin is dry and bumpy. Its legs are short, so it can only hop, not leap. And toads spend more of their time on land than frogs do.

LEARN MORE! READ THESE ARTICLES…
AMPHIBIANS (VOLUME 11) • MARSHES (VOLUME 1)
SWAMPS (VOLUME 1)

The tree frog has long legs and sticky sucker-like disks on its feet for climbing.
© Darren Maybury—Eye Ubiquitous/Corbis

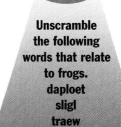

SEARCH LIGHT

Unscramble the following words that relate to frogs.
daploet
sligl
traew

Answer: daploet = tadpole
sligl = gills
traew = water

G L O S S A R Y

abdomen the end portion of an insect's body that is behind the head and thorax (middle section)

abyssal having to do with an area of the ocean that is thousands of metres below the surface of the water

adaptation change in an organism or its parts that allows the organism to survive better in its environment

algae (singular: alga) group of organisms that are similar to plants and live mostly in the water

antenna (plural: antennae) long slender organ on the head of an insect that allows it to sense its environment

bask to lie or relax in a warm place

bray to make a sound like the loud harsh call of a donkey

bushman in Australia, a person who lives in the bush (wilderness)

camouflage colours and patterns that allow a person, animal, or thing to blend in with the surroundings

captivity taken and held in a cage or as a prisoner

carcass dead body or leftover parts of an animal

colony in biology, a group of similar organisms that live together in a particular place

contour the outline of a figure, body, or surface

contract (verb) to make smaller by tightening or squeezing together

crest standing clump of fur or feathers, usually on an animal's head

digestive system parts of the body that work together to break down food into simpler forms that can be used by the body

echo (verb) to repeat or imitate a sound

evolve to change, especially over time

flare (verb) to fan out or expand

gills pair of breathing organs found in fish and some other water-dwelling animals

gland structure in animals that produces special substances, such as sweat or oil or milk

hatch to come forth from an egg or other protective covering during development

hibernate to pass the winter in a sleeping or resting state

impish playfully naughty

larva (plural: larvae) wingless, often wormlike stage of many insects

lung organ that helps some animals breathe air

majestic grand or splendid

meal coarsely ground substance

migration movement from one country or place to another

mineral substance that is not animal or plant and is an important nutrient for living things

nectar sweet liquid produced by plants and used by bees in making honey

nocturnal active at night

nuisance annoying or troublesome person, thing, or event

nutrient substance that a living thing needs in order to stay healthy and grow

pied (adjective) having blotches of two or more colours

plate in the Earth sciences, a large segment of the Earth's crust (outer layer) that is constantly in motion

pollen very fine dusty substance that comes from flowers; it is important in the reproduction of plants

prey animal eaten by another animal

savage extremely violent

scale one of the small stiff flat plates that form an outer covering on the body of some animals, especially fishes and reptiles

scorpion animal of the arachnid class (which includes spiders) that has a long body and a narrow sectioned tail with a poisonous stinger at the tip

snout long projecting nose, like that of a pig; also, the long front part of the head of some animals, such as alligators

squid sea mollusc that has a long thin body with eight short arms and two usually longer tentacles

sturdy physically strong and healthy

suction holding onto something by sucking

superstition unproven belief usually based on a mistaken idea of how something is caused

tentacle long arm-like structure on certain animals, usually found sticking out near the head or mouth and used especially for feeling or grasping

thorax the middle of the three main divisions of the body of an insect

tropical having to do with the Earth's warmest and most humid (moist) climates

unique very unusual or one-of-a-kind

vegetarian person or animal that does not eat meat

venom poison that comes from animals

vibrate to move rapidly back and forth or from side to side

warm-blooded having a body temperature that stays mostly unchanged and is not affected by the surrounding environment

waterproof not affected by water